IN
THE
Midst
OF
THIS

What to Do While You Are Still Going Through

HERTISTINE WASHINGTON

Published by Inspire Books
www.inspire-books.com

Cover and Interior Design by Jose Pepito
Inspire Books

Print ISBN: 978-1-961065-34-5
Ebook ISBN: 978-1-961065-35-2

Printed in the United States

Dedication

*This book is dedicated to everyone who
is still going through something.*

I am aware some people might think they already know what to do while they are still going through, and for this reason, they may think they don't need to read *In the Midst of This*. What I would say to them is, praise God for His revelation to you! I'm simply hoping that *In the Midst of This* will shed even more of God's empowering light on your situation and will encourage you further to keep on keeping on in Christ.

Contents

Acknowledgment

First, above all, I thank God for all He's done in my life. All glory to His name. Without Him, I can do nothing.

I thank my wonderful husband, Harvest, who is my life's love and has been my main encouragement and support, co-authoring with me on our journey. I'm so grateful for your patience and enduring love for me, which has helped and inspired me to see this work to completion.

I thank my most accomplished publisher, Beth Lottig of Inspire Books, for her much encouragement and support in helping to get this book out to everyone.

I appreciate my dear family and close friends for their continual inspiration, support, and encouragement, which have helped me through some difficult and challenging moments in my life.

I thank God for my pastor, Dr. George E. Hurtt (pastor of Mt. Sinai Church of LA), for teaching me to remain steadfast, unmovable, and to always abound in the work of the Lord.

I thank God for being a member of the Power of P.E.N.S. (Prayer, Expression, Networking & Support) Writers' group.

I also thank and appreciate you, the readers of this book and the sharers of this book. Without you, I would be writing to myself. So thank you for taking the time to pick up a copy and share with someone else.

Introduction

I began writing this book during the pandemic on December 13, 2020. This was when God put into my heart to title it *In the Midst of This*. Although this was an extremely difficult time for our country and world, we, as Christians, still held to the fact that God was still in control of what was going on. For sure, He brought the world through that devastating time.

Now that the pandemic is over, on many levels, life can still be challenging as we know it. No ifs, ands, or buts about it. For certain, there will be difficult moments in this thing call life. Some may ignorantly wonder if God created a world with so much pain, suffering, and hardship. I hope you are not one of those who think that way. If so, let me put your mind at ease: God didn't create a world of trouble and pain. He created a beautiful world in every way. Here's a flashback of what God did in the beginning.

In the beginning, God created the man, Adam, in a holy and happy state and placed him in a lovely, perfect garden home with no issues of suffering or hardships of any kind. Well, you may ask, where did the suffering and hardship come from? They came because of sin. They came when Adam disobeyed

God in his perfect environment, breaking his sweet fellowship with Him.

This caused Adam to live in a fallen state in a fallen world of hardships and sufferings brought on by his sin of disobedience. Because of his disobedience, troubling times fell on him and the entire human race. Yet, in the process of time, *in the midst of this*, God did something miraculous. He sent His one and only Son, Jesus, to restore Adam/man's relationship back with Him.

So Jesus came and took on the penalty of sin for us. None of us, and no one before us, met the qualification for paying the penalty of sin's eradication. Only Jesus. He rooted out and done away with the penalty that sin had over us by way of *His* suffering and dying on the cross and rising from the dead.

Therefore, sin has been paid for. So if sin has been paid for, why do we still experience times of hardship and pain? This is a question many still wonder about because of a lack of knowledge of God's Word. God's Word possesses the answers to all our questions.

Although the penalty of sin has been paid for, God's Word reminds us that all have sinned and come short of the glory of God (Romans 3:23). Mind you, we are still in this fallen world, but repentance through believing in the shed blood of Jesus makes it possible to restore our relationship back with God. Sin no longer has control over us. Jesus made that possible.

Also, God's Word further reminds us that in this world, we will have trials and tribulations and tough times (John 16:33). However, not all challenging or difficult times we go through are a result of sin. They are a part of life. No one is excluded from experiencing them. But be aware sin is trouble, and when we continue to dabble in sin, we will find trouble, and trouble will be ours.

With that said, the only record to help us realize why we could be going through what we are going through is found in God's Word. Know that His Word states facts, not assumptions, assuring us we can trust the guidance of the Holy Spirit to reveal the reality of God's purpose in our situation.

As David said, "The steps of a man are established by the LORD, when he delights in his way; though he fall, he shall not be cast headlong, for the LORD upholds his hand" (Psalm 37:23–24). What a promise! A promise that regardless of what we are going through, Jesus is right there in the midst to provide sustaining power.

In the Midst of This reveals what we can do to endure the hardest of life's challenging moments. It encourages us to remain steadfast in believing prayer, praise, and worship that Jesus is there to help us get through what can be overwhelming at times. The psalmist said, "Hear my cry, O God, listen to my prayer; from the end of the earth I call to you when my heart is faint. Lead me to the rock that is higher than I" (Psalm 61:1–2).

Not only that, he reminds us, "When the cares of my heart are many, your consolations cheer my soul" (Psalm 94:19). I hope these scriptures encourage you despite what you're still going through. Hopefully, they will help you to maintain your faith, trust, hope, and patience to wait on God and know that He can give you the strength needed to continue steadfast. Remember, there is nothing impossible with God.

So when we realize we have a Big God in the midst of this, our troubles will not seem so insurmountable. Again, the

Scripture bares record: "The LORD your God is in your midst, a mighty one who will save; he will rejoice over you with gladness; he will quiet you by his love; he will exult over you with loud singing" (Zephaniah 3:17). Therefore, *In the Midst of This* contains godly principles that will help us gear up in order to get through while we are *still* going through. It will encourage us to know we have Someone to help us in the midst of troubled times as we struggle to see our way through.

Please note these principles are not gained from the world's view of how to get through during difficult times. They come from an unwavering and undying faith in the Lord Jesus Christ, who is able to keep us from falling. For certain, life goes on, and we should seek a way to live and deal with it that will strengthen us, be helpful to others, and upmost be glorifying to God.

The Perspective This Book Explores

Most have heard the expression, "When life hands us lemons, we should make lemonade." Well, as easy and simple as that statement implies, suppose we don't know how to make lemonade? For sure, to get a great, refreshing glass of lemonade, knowing how to balance the ingredients is very important.

Just as too much sugar and not enough water will make a horrible glass, too few lemons can disrupt the genuine taste of a glass of lemonade. To put it briefly, this book is not about making lemonade in the midst of our trying times. But it is about using godly principles that will help us gear up before and during those most difficult times when life throws us lemons.

As you can see, this is not a huge book. That was my intention for it not to be. I didn't want you to think of your problems to be insurmountable by writing you a great BIG book with a lot of "do this, do that, and the other." I want you to know that whatever you are going through can be smaller than this book you are holding in your hands (when viewed from God's perspective) and that you have the power to endure by maintaining your trust in the Almighty power of God. As 1 John 4:4 reminds us, "Little children, you are from God and have overcome them, for he who is in you is greater than he who is in the world."

So if you think your situation is big, then it can seem that way for you. Then again, if you think you are bigger than your situation, you are not. Only God is. In light of this: *In the Midst of This is not intended to minimize or make light of anyone's situation, condition, or plight. It is solely meant to encourage you that despite how small or big your situation is, God is in the midst of it to sustain you.*

Permit me to say when we think our situation is bigger than God, herein lies the problem. There is nothing bigger than God. So by gearing up in the principles of God's Word there is help available for us to get through it. In short, this book is about using God's perspective on what to do while we are *still* going through stuff—big, small, lingering, or all-of-a-sudden kinda *stuff.*

Inspiration for This Book

I don't know how God speaks to you, but I've been paying attention how He speaks to me by way of His Holy Spirit. One of the ways is by consistent confirmation. On occasions, I find His revelation to be so clear that I would have to be blind to miss it. Therefore, I've learned to ask, look, and expect God's confirmation in a matter before jumping into it, such as publishing this book, *In the Midst of This*. Thus, because of God's constant confirmation in my life from hearing a particular phrase, I was inspired to write this book.

Just as the World Health Organization (WHO) on March 11, 2020, had declared the novel coronavirus (COVID-19) outbreak a global pandemic, which produced a pause around the world because of its deadly effects, I found I had allowed the pandemic to produce a pause in my life, especially on writing, amongst other things. I must admit, like many others, I became captivated by the news of the day's happenings. I was glued to the tube, focusing on the news.

Then again, there came a time when I sensed the Lord speaking in my spirit in a still, small voice to the effect of, *"You're focusing too much on the pandemic news instead of the Good News."* That was the thought coming over my spiritual airways because that was what I was doing. In view of that constant thought, I stopped watching so much pandemic news and began focusing more on the spiritual news of God.

It happened one day as I was taking notes from my favorite television evangelist when I heard something that got my attention. But first, let me share this: My husband shared in the foreword section of my previous book (*Sacred and Intimate Lives of Husbands and Wives*) how I am always taking and writing notes. Well, again, this little book came about when I was just writing notes.

On that day, I was listening to an evangelist as he expounded on trusting God. Of the many things he elaborated on, one phrase stood out in my mind. He said quickly, "In the midst of this." It was this phrase that got stuck in my ear, although he only said it once.

On another occasion, I heard it in a prayer while someone was praying. There it was again: "in the midst of this." Still, later on, someone made a post on social media about leaning and depending on God—get this—"in the midst of." There the phrase was again. Three times in one week was enough for me to take notice. By the end of that week, it was rooted in my thoughts.

Early the next morning, as I was reading and meditating, I heard it again, but this time in my spirit. Here's the thing: Prior to that week, an ongoing painful matter had become worse in our family involving a loved one, which was getting better before the pandemic occurred.

As countless can witness, while the pandemic continued having its damaging affect around the world in social distance, it was not surprising that many found it extremely difficult to adjust to this new way of coping. To say the least, in various ways my own state of mind/well-being was impacted. Having said that, one of our loved ones fell into a severe crisis trying to cope during this devastating period. Seeing that the situation was not letting up, my family and I went to God in honest and sincere prayer. Finally, I prayed, "Lord, in the midst of this, please help us! Show us what to do while we are still going through." Thus, praying that simple prayer ignited this book.

This book shares what I believe God told me to do while we were still going through that very difficult time. At this point of writing, *In the Midst of This*, we are still faced with this family struggle—however, not in despair, but with hope. Having shared this, I would like to ask you to consider the following question.

What Are You Still Going Through?

What are you in the midst of right now? Think about it. What do you wish you could fix right now? What's worrying you? What's on your mind? What struggle or crisis are you in? Could it be if you begin writing what is really troubling you, you may still be writing? The list could be endless.

Just saying, it makes no difference who we are; we all are going through something. However, there is a method to the madness. There is a method of what to do while we're still going through stuff. And yes, I sometimes refer to my challenges as "stuff" (as previously mentioned) because we all go through different stuff. Sometimes, it's hard to clarify, but it's still stuff, when viewed from God's perspective.

In light of our current world situation, many may be thinking, "We have a mess on our hands! What is the remedy? Who can fix this chaos?" Despite what you and I are personally going through, we are still living in a time with the aftereffects of a worldwide pandemic in one form or the other.

As you can witness, our government seems to be coming unraveled on every level. Our mental health crisis has become extremely evident. Also, there are prevailing economic concerns as well as much civil unrest still plaguing our streets and our world. And here we are, right in the midst of this! Where do we go? Whom do we call?

For this reason, I ask: What are you still going through? What is the answer or remedy while we're still going through these disturbing and uncertain seasons?

CHAPTER 1

In the Midst of—BAM!

Have you ever experienced your life going so smoothly and then, all of a sudden—BAM! Have you ever gone through a BAM moment, or maybe you're in one now? These are moments I characterize as making me feel suddenly "Bad And Miserable." These are not merely the regular, everyday challenges we face, but these are the unexpected, out-of-the-blue, unimaginable, unforeseen, surprising, hurtful moments that could occur all of a sudden in our lives.

Even though they may happen without warning, their effects can sometimes be drawn out and lingering. These are moments in life that can hit all of us like a tornado! It can make us want to crawl in a hole and cover our heads until that bad and miserable moment has passed. But as much as we would like to crawl in a hole, we cannot escape it by ourselves.

If you have not had one of these moments occur in your life, you are indeed a rare breed. But for those of us who have experienced this, we know that they can leave us beyond tears, feeling helpless, shaken, and alone. It can be very shocking and leave us quivering in our boots!

If you find yourself in the midst of this, or something you've never imagined could happen in a million years, you might have encountered a BAM moment. It hits like a brick. You may find yourself looking for answers and asking yourself questions: *Do I deserve this? Where did this come from? How can I fix it?* Then, to dig this hole of despair deeper, you may wonder: *What did I do wrong?*

Afterward, you may think, *I followed all the rules. How could I have not seen this coming?* Or *how could this possibly happen to me?*! It appears most of our wondering tends to point back to "I" in BAM moments.

Finding ourselves being overwhelmed by questions like these, inquiring minds may want to know how can "I" survive this bad and miserable moment. How can "I" get through it? To answer this, I hope you realize many times "I" may have nothing to do with it. Life happens. But for those who have come to know Christ, know that God is not pleased in us simply wallowing in our troubles, crying our eyes out, nursing our problems, and letting them take control of us. When BAM moments occur, there are ways to get through without succumbing to them.

Are you aware there are biblical patriarchs (men and women) to help us with the BAM moments of life? Some found themselves in what I would consider a super-duper BAM moment despite their faith and hope in God. What they did in those BAM moments got them through it.

Just to mention a few: Though being a man of consistent prayer, Daniel found himself in the lion's den, subjected to being devoured by them (Daniel 6). BAM! Jeremiah, being a man of faithful preaching, found himself shut off in the deepest, darkest of dungeons (Jeremiah 38). BAM!

Let's take a look at Esther. She was a brave and strong queen who risked her life in approaching King Xerxes in hopes of saving the entire nation of Israel. Could that have been Esther's BAM moment? It could very well have been. For no one went into the king unannounced and without risking their life. Through that BAM moment, God granted her favor with the king (Esther 1–10) by granting her request.

What about Deborah, a judge and warrior for ancient Israel, who led Israel to victory against their enemy? I imagine every time she went on the battlefield, she did it at a risk to her own life. It was her love for God and His people that kept her faithfully pursuing the enemy in battle (Judges 4 and 5).

Lest we forget, Brother Job, an upright and righteous man who found himself one day losing all he had: possessions gone, children dead, wife about to lose it, and now himself, lying in a bed covered with sores (Job 1). Oh my, BAM!

Now let me ask you: What do you think helped those men and women get through their BAM experiences? I believe being geared up with godly principles—such as prayer, faith, hope, patience, strength, and constant communion with God—sustained them through it all.

Then again, someone may ask: Those patriarchs got through their BAM moments alive, but what about John the Baptist, Jesus's very own earthy cousin? He didn't get through alive. He was beheaded! My response would be, yes, he was beheaded, but not for doing wrong—instead, it was for speaking out against wrong for the cause of Christ.

John the Baptist's experience brought to my mind God didn't promise we wouldn't lose our lives; however, He did promise "whoever loses his life for my sake will find it" (Matthew 10:39). I believe John was willing to take the risk for Christ for eternal "new life" in Him. No, John didn't physically survive through his physical BAM moment, but he did endure it by maintaining his faith and trust in Christ to gain eternal life in Him. No, John didn't lose, he gained. Also, read Hebrews chapter 11. You'll find countless others who endured BAM moments for the cause of Christ.

As you may now have become aware, through the ups and downs of the patriarchs' BAM moments, they held on to their faith. They all had something better to look forward to than what they were still going through and were willing to die for it. They had a hope (Hebrews chapter 8)—hope that one day, a better day in Christ would come. What am I saying? If we keep our eyes on Jesus, He will also give us the hope and strength to bear the BAM moments of our lives.

You may wonder if such faith exists today. God only knows. Hopefully, our tests or trials in life do not have to be as severe as John's or any of these brave men and women of faith. But, to be a follower of Christ, we can also have BAM moments occur that will challenge our faith.

Question: How do we hold on after being hit with—BAM? One way is by having a good view of Christ and knowing how He suffered through it all for us. This can make the difference in whether we will endure—or not. For this reason, I hope we hold on to our faith when faced with the most unforeseen challenges of our lives.

I'm aware most of us just want our *stuff* or our *this* to go away, disappear, or vanish. Unfortunately, that is not how life happens. Know that these kinds of thoughts tend to pop up when we find ourselves at our wits' end in a BAM (Bad And Miserable) situation. I'm thanking God experiencing a BAM moment doesn't have to define my state of living. There is something we can do when we find ourselves encountering what can be a completely shocking moment.

Would you believe, right at finishing this section on BAM, I mistakenly hit a button on my computer that caused not only that part of my rough draft to disappear but also another section? Then there it was—BAM! I thought, *Really, Lord*? I felt bad and miserable for a moment because, as hard as I tried, I couldn't retrieve the information back.

But thanks be to God—before my material vanished, I remembered sending a copy to my email. Therefore, I was able to refresh my page. Hallelujah! The devil is a liar! Even though this may not have been classified as a severe BAM moment to some, it was definitely one for me!

I shared that simple experience because occasionally when we least expect it, *in the midst of this,* a BAM could easily exist. The question is, then, what to do when they do. Brace yourselves—Again, here it is. *The way to get through while we are still going through is to become familiar with and apply certain godly principles found in God's Word.* Being aware of these godly principles can help us make ready before, during, and after sudden moments of BAM!

Hopefully, having read this first chapter, you have gained confidence to know BAM moments don't have to destroy you. They don't have to take you out! You can survive after a BAM moment if you hold on to your faith in God. I'm not saying it's easy, but with Christ, it can be done. Remember His yoke is easy, and His burden is light (Matthew 11:30). So let us praise Him for His help to endure those unexpected, unforeseen, unknowable, and out-of-the-blue challenging moments.

I pray as you read further, you will be encouraged to also know that our trials, situations, and experiences can lead us into a new and different, yet deeper relationship with God. Let us appreciate the truth that God not only stands on the outside of our situations, He also is there with us in the midst of them to sustain us, even when life says . . . BAM!

In the Midst of This, in Times of BAM!

What then shall we say to these things? If God is for us, who can be against us?

—Romans 8:31

When you pass through the waters, I will be with you; and through the rivers, they shall not overwhelm you; when you walk through fire you shall not be burned, and the flame shall not consume you.

—Isaiah 43:2

Beloved, do not be surprised at the fiery trial when it comes upon you to test you, as though something strange were happening to you.

—1 Peter 4:12

CHAPTER 2

Gear Up in Your Gear

F irst of all, are you aware life is an everyday gearing up, whether we are going through something or not? Every day, we gear up for something. In the mornings as we get out of bed, we begin by gearing up for the day. We gear up in our dress. We gear up for a hearty breakfast, all in preparation for the day. Many take morning meds and exercise to gear up for health and endurance.

Just as the teacher gears up to prepare the lessons for the students, the preacher gears up to bring God's Word to the congregation. Just as the employee gears up for the work, the employer gears up to see that the work is done. There are many others who gear up to make ready for the tasks ahead. Lest we forget, we also gear up for the fun side of life. We gear up for vacations, trips, special events, and sometimes for needed rest and relaxation.

I hope you understand from these few examples that gearing up in the midst of life is a big, continual part of life. So if we know that gearing up is a part of everyday life, how important do we think it is to practice gearing up for the major challenges life can bring?

Are you aware in difficult moments, many people give up instead of gearing up? Are you also aware many stop doing the needful thing that may help them to press through the very thing they are struggling with? That being said, when life throws us a blow, we still need to gear up. Let us not throw our hands up in the midst of this but gear up instead for what may lie ahead.

Sometimes when trouble comes our way out of nowhere, many of us tend to draw up or try to fight it with our own strength. Sometimes, I think we forget we have gear—gear that will enable us, in the midst of this, to withstand the most difficult challenges.

Do you know that we as Christians have a special kind of gear that will help us to get through the everyday challenges we face? But first, let's see what it means to gear up. To "gear up" is to prepare or equip oneself for something, get ready, make preparation before an act or situation occurs or even during an ongoing situation. In other words, we should never stop gearing up. As we can see now, there are many situations in life that call for us to gear up.

Our country, our world, already has things set in place for possible unforeseeable demands or attacks that would limit or prevent impending danger or catastrophes. By doing this, they are not expecting chaos to happen, but have made ready in case it does. As our country is aware of the urgency to gear up or make preparation before such things could take place, so should we as Christians in our physical and spiritual life gear up so that we, too, may be able to withstand in the midst of life's hardships.

Gearing Up for Battle

Making preparation for war is one example to show how important it is to gear up. My husband, being a Vietnam veteran, would tell me stories about his comrades and how they had to gear up before actually engaging in the act of war. Everyone had to have and be responsible for their own gear.

Each soldier had to gear up in their gear before they would be ready to engage in an attack. They had to be ready to face the moment in the moment. For the enemy could be lurking anywhere. They understood that if they waited to gear up during the crucial moment their enemy was on the attack, it could possibly be too late to survive. Training time would be over. It was time to fight.

Being mindful of that, one very important component that helped them to be successful in their fight was their gear. It needed to be right in its fit and in its weight. They were to wear it, walk with it, sleep with it, and always keep it on or near their person.

Again, the danger was no one knew when the enemy was to strike. They had to be ready. If a soldier didn't have his proper gear, he subjected himself to being overtaken by his opponent and be possibly killed on the battlefield. Therefore, a soldier had to be equipped for war in a critical time, even when war was not imminent.

We, as Christians, may not be in a physical army, but we certainly are living in critical times, for wars are happening on many levels. Initially, as I mentioned, when I began writing this book, the world was experiencing a global pandemic war. Not to mention socioeconomic wars, domestic wars, political wars, medical wars, civil wars, and mental wars. Also in light of the pandemic, other wars may have become evident in your own life as a result of these types of worldly conflicts.

As many Christians may know so well, spiritual wars can be most dangerous and challenging, with the most unseen kind of attack. They come to siege our mind and spirit. Encountering them, we may not know when something will break out or when the enemy will come upon us. We need to be equipped for the battle, so we may not be overtaken when the enemy strikes.

It goes well to say every Christian who has accepted the Lord Jesus as their personal Savior has signed up to be a soldier in God's army. The odds are they have participated in spiritual warfare at some time on some level. For a Christian, engaging in spiritual warfare is a given. With that, every Christian needs to know how to properly gear up for spiritual warfare (before and even during) to also face spiritually challenging times.

Gearing Up with the Armor of God

Understanding how a regular soldier was expected to handle his gear, I admonish we do likewise. This caused me to think about the difference in a regular soldier's gear as opposed to the kind Christians wear. Even though they both require gear, they are not worn the same way.

A regular soldier wears his gear on the outside: his shield, buckler, uniform, hat, bulletproof vest, shoes, and weapon. But a Christian wears their gear on the inside. Yes, Christians gear up from within. This is where preparation takes place when encountering the BAM moments, potholes, struggles, storms, or any lingering hardships of life.

So as we become knowledgeable of this, let us gear up in our gear. This gear will not only help us live a better physical life but also will help us combat the evil forces that attempt to invade our minds and spirits. All we need to do is simply put on our gear from the inside. At this point, you may be wondering what is the Christian gear?

A Christian's gear is the armor of God. You'll be glad to know it's one-size-fits-all! Ephesians 6:11–18 tells us of this armor:

> *Put on the whole armor of God, that you may be able to stand against the schemes of the devil. For we do not wrestle against flesh and blood, but against the rulers, against the authorities, against the cosmic powers over this present darkness, against the spiritual forces of evil in the heavenly places. Therefore take up the whole armor of God, that you may be able to withstand in the evil day, and having done all, to stand firm. Stand therefore, having fastened on the belt of truth, and having put on the breastplate of righteousness, and, as shoes for your feet, having put on the readiness given by the gospel or peace. In all circumstances take up the shield of faith, with*

> *which you can extinguish all the flaming darts of*
> *the evil one; and take the helmet of salvation, and*
> *the sword of the Spirit, which is the word of God,*
> *praying at all times in the Spirit, with all prayer*
> *and supplication.*

With everything that's going on in the world today and in our lives, I suggest we gear up in the armor of God. Wearing this armor, *In the Midst of This*, is fully effective while we are still going through.

In the Midst of This, Gear Up in Your Armor

Count it all joy, my brothers, when you meet tri-als of various kinds, for you know that the testing of your faith produces steadfastness.

—James 1:2

No, in all these things we are more than conquer-ors through him who loved us.

—Romans 8:37

I have said these things to you, that in me you may have peace. In the world you will have tribu-lation. But take heart; I have overcome the world.

—John 16:33

CHAPTER 3

Gear Up in Prayer

N ow that we have our armor on, the first principle that will be effective while we're still going through is prayer. We need to gear up in prayer. Prayer is important. It is how we talk to God. It is our spiritual telephone line to our Master's ear. There is no need to dial Him up, click, or tap a number. Simply call from your heart. He'll know it's you.

Are you aware Jesus prayed? I ask that question because someone may not know that Jesus, still being King of Kings and Lord of Lords, actually prayed. From the spiritual sense, it would seem like He wouldn't need to pray, but He did. Remember, Jesus became as much a man as He is God. So yes, our true living God prayed. While still in His humanity, He prayed to His Father while He was going through some moments, and so should we.

Are you also aware in John chapter 12, Jesus prayed a prayer so significant to securing our salvation prior to going to the cross? In His humanity, He prayed: "Now is my soul troubled.

And what shall I say? 'Father, save me from this hour'? But for this purpose, I have come to this hour" (John 12:27).

I pray you understand Jesus knew His purpose, and in His humanity, He prayed to gear Himself up to face His upcoming crucifixion. What a wonderful example for us today when we encounter what seem to be overwhelming obstacles. As Jesus gained strength by praying before facing the cross, we also can be strengthened through prayer to withstand the crosses in our lives.

Another time, Jesus prayed in John 12:28, "Father, glorify your name." Wow! When we are going through something, how many of us literally think to pray, "Father, glorify your name," in our situation? If we are honest with ourselves, some of us don't think to do this, if at all. After reading *In the Midst of This*, I hope during our trials we become more God-conscious to ask Him to manifest His glorify in our difficult situations.

We also must be mindful when facing hardships to not let the focus of our circumstances override what the will of the Lord is. His name is to be glorified above all. Pray His will be done. I am fully aware sometimes this can be easier said than done. Actually, it has been done! Simply look at Jesus. Look toward the cross! Jesus, through His agonizing pain, glorified God while being crucified on the cross.

Of course, we are not Jesus. He is God. No one will be able to suffer like He suffered. We suffer on behalf of Christ, not as the Christ. And it is He who gives us what we need to press on while suffering. He provides the strength to glorify Him in the midst of what we are going through. So please don't let the devil's lies weigh you down by believing you can't glorify God in the midst of your struggles. It can be done when you lift your mind toward Jesus.

Pray While Going Through

I further want to encourage you to gear up in your prayer life while still going through, as a result of the BAMs of life. Pray that when they happen, you will have His strength to draw on. To do this, you need to increase your dialogue with God. Make it a practice to talk to Him every day, morning, noon, evening, and night. Believe, believe, believe God is working in the midst of your situation. He can make everything all right according to His will for your life and His glory.

For this reason, I urge you to continue to gear up in sincere prayer by thanking God as you pray to Him. For sure, thanking Him is a good way to pray. Thank Him for being who He is. Thank Him for what He has done. Thank Him for listening and helping you. Also thank Him for relinquishing that excruciating pain, that unimaginable hurt, that physical, medical, or mental anguish you may have been going through. Thank Him for His peace and comfort.

Furthermore, if you are still going through these challenges, thank Him for continuing to hold you up. In light of this, do you believe prayer changes things? It seems if we really believed this, we would pray more. Like the popular hymn says, "Have we trials and temptations? Is there trouble anywhere? Take it to the Lord in prayer." Yes, remembering to take all our cares to the Lord in prayer is definitely a good way to pray while going through.

I pray as you build your relationship of prayer with God you can confidently pray, "Father, thank you for hearing my prayer." I pray you are confident He did hear you because of your special relationship with Him through prayer and that you have not made yourself a stranger through lack of prayer but a friend through constant prayer.

In the Midst of This, Gear Up in Prayer

Do not be anxious about anything, but in everything by prayer and supplication with thanksgiving let your requests be made known to God. And the peace of God, which surpasses all understanding, will guard your hearts and your minds in Christ Jesus.

—Philippians 4:6-7

Rejoice in hope, be patient in tribulation, be constant in prayer.

—Romans 12:12

In my distress I called upon the LORD; to my God I cried for help. From his temple he heard my voice, and my cry to him reached his ears.

—Psalm 18:6

CHAPTER 4

Gear up in Worship and Praise

How deep is your worship? How high is your praise? Clearly, there is no number to measure the height of our praise nor the depth of our worship. We simply worship and praise God from a sincere heart. To worship God is to worship Him for who He is, His very character, His very nature. To worship God is to worship Him in spirit and in truth. To praise God is to praise Him for what He has done, is doing, and for what He can and will do.

Understanding these two differences or meanings gives us reason to praise God to the highest of heights and to worship Him to the deepest of depths from a sincere heart. If we're truthful, we can all stand to gear up in our worship and praise to Him. God is so deserving.

God's Word tells us in Matthew 26:41 "the spirit indeed is willing, but the flesh is weak." With this verse I don't believe Jesus is making an excuse for the flesh in that we can't do for

Him because of it. I believe Jesus is actually getting rid of the excuses for the flesh.

Are you aware this can also be true in reference to our worship and praise? Sometimes, we make excuses because our flesh gets tired. And (true enough) our flesh does get tired, but still, there is no excuse not to give God the worship and praise due His name. Know that God has given us of His Holy Spirit to override the desires of our flesh.

I'm still learning it is so important to gear up in worship and praise, even in the midst of physical tiredness or fatigue. It is true our flesh doesn't desire to worship God at all and absolutely cannot. For this reason, we praise God for giving us His Spirit to overpower and keep our flesh under subordination. If we worship enough, I'm pretty confident we won't allow our flesh to handle us any kind of way. Sure, it's only human to get tired sometimes, but when the Spirit urges us to pray, we should be careful not to let our flesh have the last say.

Have you ever allowed your flesh to override your spirit in the midst of what you were going through? I'm sure the best of us have been fooled by listening to the advice of our fleshly nature at one time or the other. When I speak of the flesh, I'm referring to our carnal nature, which is self-willed, self-focused, and self-seeking.

The Flesh Can Sabotage Our Praise

Do you know when we allow our flesh to fool us by telling us we are too tired and weak, we can become spiritually sabotaged in our worship and praise? May I just add when we don't feel like worshipping and praising God, we could find ourselves easily influenced by the flesh. Just saying, have you ever been spiritually distracted in your worship and praise? I'm not saying you actually stopped worshipping God. For we know He is God, and He only is to be worshipped.

Maybe I should ask more specifically: Has there been a situation or hardship to occur in your life that you may have found yourself being steered slightly off course in some way from your praise and worship of God by focusing more on the hardship you were facing? I admit it happened to me. Not making any excuse, but my lack of focus happened during one of the most challenging times in our history, the pandemic of 2019.

At that time, I should have allowed my spirit to have the final say regarding making some choices, not my flesh. In other words, I ought to have been more watchful of the enemy's sabotaging influence during that particular time in my life. The Bible lets us know the enemy comes only to steal, kill, and destroy (John 10:10). As you might guess, I'm so thankful he didn't kill me or destroy me. But because of my lack of watchfulness, I had allowed him to steal from me during that most difficult time in history by undermining my worship and praise.

This came to light when I was blessed with an opportunity to participate with our church in The Daniel Fast during the time of this pandemic. As such, I titled the following segment "A Fast Food Find."

A Fast Food Find

As mentioned, my Fast Food Find happened during the COVID-19 pandemic when I participated in the Daniel Fast at my church. This was from January 4 through January 15, 2021.

For those who may not know, The Daniel Fast is based on the book of Daniel, which states in Daniel 10:3, "I ate no delicacies, no meat or wine entered my mouth, nor did I anoint myself at all, for the full three weeks." This Daniel Fast involved a decision that Daniel made to deprive himself of pleasant food, meat, and wine for three weeks while he sought God in prayer.

As you can gather from the above date, our church had begun this fast about nine months after the Governor of California initially had declared a shutdown, a "Stay at Home Order" for the state of California in March of 2020. This "Stay at Home Order" was enforced because of the widespread deadly and damaging health effects of the Coronavirus outbreak.

After being in shutdown for several months and trying to move on after the shutdown ended, the Daniel Fast became a welcomed experience for me. You see, I had developed some unhealthy habits during the shutdown that were continuing in my life even after the shutdown was over, but not the pandemic.

During this time, I experienced some challenging moments in trying to move forward, as I believed most people did. That being said, I was excited about participating in the Daniel Fast for a couple of reasons. First, I felt by participating God was calling me back to a path I had somewhat deferred from while the shutdown was in effect. That path consisted of the quantity of time I spent in worship and praise. I had become a bit spiritually sluggish.

During the fast, I was surprised to see just how far I had slacked up from worshipping and praising God, as I had before the shutdown began. Secondly, I wanted to feel whole again as I did before the pandemic began. I felt I needed to get back on track with God in my worship and praise while still in the midst of the pandemic. Mind you, after the COVID-19 shutdown, I had problems getting back to my "self," as I was. Trying to adjust to the pandemic's shutdown all the while dealing with my loved one's struggle to cope during this period, in the midst of this, I also felt my emotional health had become somewhat impacted. I knew something was off with me. Actually, I felt a bit discombobulated. Not making an excuse. Simply stating a fact. So if you also got somewhat perplexed during this time, maybe you can relate.

I didn't realize at the onset of the shutdown how I had allowed it to affect my worship and praise. Although I was still praying and reading my Bible, I became neglectful in the quantity and quality of time I did, despite literally having more time to do so at home.

I used much of my time for cleaning when I wanted to clean (no rush, no deadline). On some days, my pajamas were my attire, and my house shoes were my footwear throughout the day. I also wasn't aware that I had let the pandemic shutdown shut me down in certain ways.

Listening to the constant updates practically every day had become my shutdown lifestyle for a while. Also scrolling social media had become my source of entertainment during the shutdown. This caused me to get into the habit of paying attention to my cell phone—a lot.

Along with that, my diet also changed. I started eating unhealthy foods: chips, cookies, cheese, fried foods, pastries, candy, and ice cream (comfy foods). Maybe you can identify?

I didn't gain a lot of weight, but my blood pressure and cholesterol were definitely affected. Realizing I wasn't feeling well, I masked up and to the doctor I went. Getting back unfavorable results, I began paying better attention to my health.

Although I had unknowingly increased my unhealthy food intake, I was also not exercising nor reading my Bible as regularly as I did before the fast. I had slacked up in getting up early and getting alone with God in worship and praise, which was once the highlight of the beginning of my day before the pandemic's shutdown.

It was moments like these that I had allowed to shift my attention off worshipping and praising God as I once did. I definitely had left some weightier things undone. So when the Daniel Fast was announced for our church, I was so thankful. I thought to myself: *Yes, this may help me get back to where I got off, to refocus my focus.*

So, after the shutdown ended, participating in the Daniel Fast came at a much-needed time in my life. You understand, some of those habits I acquired during the pandemic shutdown I was still allowing to affect me nine months after. Becoming aware of this, I was determined and hopeful to use the Daniel Fast to get *me* back in focus spiritually and health-wise.

All I can say is thank God for the wake-up call! I can't say it enough; it's good to realize you are off track and even better to know what is needed to get back on track. I am so thankful to God in the midst of this pandemic for helping me to gear down in my bad eating habits and to gear up in foods that helped strengthen me in my worship and praise of God again.

As I indicated, the kinds of foods I was consuming had affected my spiritual state and frame of mind. I was tired most mornings, even after sleeping all night. Get that, will ya! This tiredness persisted. As mentioned, I began to realize this during the Daniel Fast. I knew a change needed to take place. I can tell you, at times I was so tired my praise would be so low that I'd wondered where did it go?!

Then, one day, I just prayed, "Lord, forgive me, please! Restore me." Thankfully, God did get me back on track to eating according to the fast and praising and thanking Him before I placed an ounce of food in my mouth. Again, as I said earlier, I had to *refocus my focus*.

You see, at first, I was so concentrated on finding the right kinds of foods for the fast that I had missed the main purpose of the fast. It is not to refrain from foods simply for the sake of not eating or just to get healthy. For me, it meant I needed to refrain from those things that were hindering or causing an interference in my relationship with God. And yes, sometimes that was food. Yet I found I needed more.

During this fast, I came to realize whatever was causing me to be neglectful in my time with God was what I needed to fast away from. Therefore, I started seeking God passionately again. In the midst of this, I pulled aside and asked the Holy Spirit what I should do or not do to get back on track in praising God wholeheartedly.

Through the Holy Spirit, I was reminded I needed to find the kinds of foods that would not only be good for my body but my soul. Realizing this through praise and worship, I began to purposely take into account what I was putting into my body and why. As I did this, the Lord was helping me to build back a closer and deeper relationship in Him.

Instead of craving for the wrong foods, I again began craving for a taste of Him in His Word early in the mornings and throughout the day as I geared back up in worship and praise. As I did this, not only my physical strength returned but also my spiritual strength. I felt strengthened in both areas.

I can joyfully say I'm so grateful God has restored back to me a healthier appetite for Him through the Daniel Fast. For sure, during this Fast Food Find, I was blessed to find the true food of His Word that I needed to nourish my soul in the midst of the pandemic. I prayed to the Lord, as in Proverbs 30:8, "Feed me with the food that is needful for me."

As a result of this, I am a whole lot better in mind, body, and spirit. I'm discovering when I deny the pleasures of my appetites for the true treasures of nourishment found in God's Word, it will ultimately result in a deeper, healthier, and closer relationship with Him in the midst of any struggle.

In the Midst of This, Gear Up in Worship and Praise

God is spirit, and those who worship him must worship in spirit and truth.

—John 4:24

O LORD, you are my God; I will exalt you; I will praise your name, for you have done wonderful things, plans formed of old, faithful and sure.

—Isaiah 25:1

I cried to him with my mouth, and high praise was on my tongue.

—Psalm 66:17

CHAPTER 5

Gear Up in the Knowledge of God

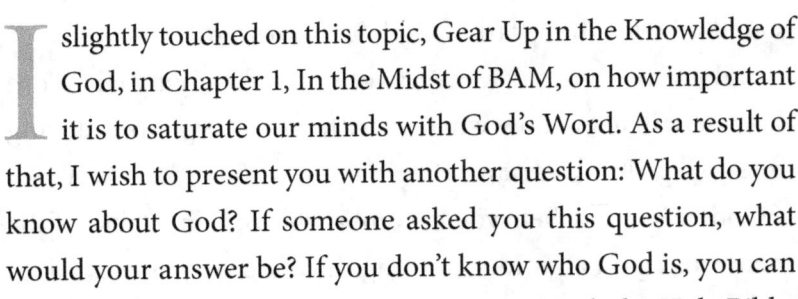

I slightly touched on this topic, Gear Up in the Knowledge of God, in Chapter 1, In the Midst of BAM, on how important it is to saturate our minds with God's Word. As a result of that, I wish to present you with another question: What do you know about God? If someone asked you this question, what would your answer be? If you don't know who God is, you can always learn of Him by reading from His Word, the Holy Bible.

I'm learning also that getting to know God calls for more than simply reading His Word. It also calls for meditating on His Word. For when we meditate, we are ushering in space for the Holy Spirit to reveal to us the very character and nature of God. Then, as we face difficult moments, we have knowledge of someone who can help us prevail. If you've never sought after God before, I pray you use this time to gear up in your knowledge of Him.

Are you familiar with the phrase, "Knowledge is power"? Most of us are. Let us keep in mind this can be so true in both the physical realm and in the spiritual realm. So you will be aware it is our spiritual knowledge that will help us stand against the enemy and his attacks. Our Lord gave us a good picture of this when he was led into the wilderness by the Spirit to be tempted of the devil. He showed us what to use when standing against the attacks of the enemy.

In His humanity, Jesus used His knowledge of God's Word to fight off the attacks of Satan after being in the wilderness for forty days and forty nights. Though being all God, yet in His humanity still all man, Jesus got hungry. To defeat Satan, He used the spiritual power of God's Word. He told Satan, "It is written." As we can see, in the midst of this temptation, Jesus geared up with the Word of God, "It is written."

Like Jesus, I encourage you to gear up in studying His Word that you will also know what is written to be equipped during times of spiritual warfare. Remind yourself of what the Word of God says. It will help you to combat the unseen attacks of the enemy and gain an understanding that God may be at work in your situation to bring His will and purpose to pass.

I'm aware sometimes things can feel so overwhelming that you may throw your hands in the air and think, *What's the use? Why, oh, why?* (Refer to the BAM Moments, Chapter 1.) For this reason, I urge you to hold on to the fact that God will never want you to give up on Him while you are still going through.

Now, the devil would love for us to give up on God. He wants us to think God has stopped working in our lives, that God has deserted us, that God may be penalizing us for some wrong we may have done. Permit me to say: We shouldn't believe the devil's lies. Let us remain confident God has the answer to our situation, and He can sustain us through it.

I hope we are more confident God has not left us alone and never will. No matter what we are going through, He's *still* in the midst with us. We can hold on to this because His Word promises: "Fear not, for I am with you; do not be dismayed, for I am your God; I will strengthen you, I will help you, I will uphold you with my righteous right hand" (Isaiah 41:10). I pray we keep God's Word in our hearts richly, that we have no doubt of His constant presence in the midst of our trails.

Even though there is no instant formula that will rid you of the shocking or lingering difficult moments of life, there is a spiritual formula to sustain you through them all—God's Word. I admonish you to gear up in His Word until it reaches your spirit. You can say God's Word repeatedly to yourself until it propels to the forefront of your mind when confronted with these unexpected or drawn-out difficult situations.

I pray you wake up knowing God already knows what life holds for you. Be secure in believing that the *omniscient, almighty, all-sufficient, all-wise* Father is already aware. He knew when trials were coming, and guess what? He allowed them to come for His purpose.

Therefore, I suggest we maintain a sound knowledge of His Word so that we gain a better understanding of His will, purpose, and wisdom during our situations. Why not encourage yourself by saying: "Despite what I'm going through, I'm going to wait and depend on God. He might be fulfilling His divine purpose in my situation."

No, we may not understand *how* He's fulfilling His purpose in our situations. We may not like *how* He does it. We may not *feel* good about it. But I dare you to trust God. The pain and hurt of your struggle may not go away right away, but God can provide comfort and strength in the midst of your hardship to endure.

I trust you understand we are not privy to all God is doing in our lives. And never will be. He doesn't take us into His confidence. We take Him in ours by trusting Him. We can be grateful God doesn't let us know all the whats, whens, wheres, or hows of our situation. He is far too wise to let us in on His plan. Consequently, I pray you will gear up in your spiritual knowledge in knowing God will never fail you.

I'm recalling a particular time I almost thought God had failed me. But praise be to the Knower of All Things—in His unique way, He comforted and assured me He was in the midst all along. I feel blessed to share how God allowed me to experience His unfailing love in such a unique way that it literally blew my mind. He did this early one morning by slowly awakening me from a dream, as the world was still in the midst of the COVID-19 pandemic.

God Never Fails

It happened one early Sunday morning at 5:00 a.m., January 10, 2021. I was in my bed, waking up from a deep sleep. My mind was alert, but my eyes were fast shut. I realized I was somewhat coming out of a dream. As I lay there, I saw an abundance of scrambled words in my unconscious mind. I couldn't see where the words were coming from, nor could I make out their meaning.

When I finally opened my unconscious eyes (still partly asleep), it appeared as if I was in the midst of this "fog," trying to wake up and make sense of what I was vaguely seeing. Wrestling to wake up, I still wasn't able to see the words clearly. I kept trying, but I couldn't because of that heavy fog that engulfed me. It seemed as if the words were putting forth their very best effort to reach me despite the thickness of the cloud of fog. They appeared to be coming through the fog in waves, like waves of the sea.

Now, as the bungle of words kept coming toward me (appearing to be surfing on these gigantic waves), I was beginning to hear sounds, though somewhat muffled. Then the sound of the words began to carry a tune—a familiar tune, I must say. I began (literally) bobbing my head up and down on my pillow, all the while trying to return to sleep. As those words were becoming louder, I began to feel, in some strange way, comforted by them.

During that feeling of comfort, I saw myself trying to focus on the words and the tune as much as possible, regardless of the heavy fog hindering my sight. The more I bobbed my head to the tune and kept trying to see through the fog, the fog slowly started evaporating.

After a while, it seemed as though the bobbling of my head to the tune was causing the fog to quickly vanish. Now, at this time, I could see the words much clearer. They were no longer scrambled. They read in big, bold capital letters: **ALL OF MY**

LIFE I'VE NEVER KNOWN YOU TO FAIL. YOU REMAIN THE SAME. WONDERFUL IS YOUR NAME! I still wasn't quite sure what was happening to me since I was coming out of a deep sleep, especially after having recently experienced a troublesome week!

Yet I heard myself repeating those words over and over again, still not completely awake. Then I understood them to be the words from a familiar song my church had often sang before the shutdown began, during the COVID-19 pandemic. Now, they seemingly were coming toward me, getting bigger by the wave. To my surprise, this familiar song was now resonating in my head at five o'clock on that morning: **ALL OF MY LIFE I'VE NEVER KNOWN YOU TO FAIL. YOU REMAIN THE SAME. WONDERFUL IS YOUR NAME!**

Those words, as I repeated them in my mind, got louder and loud, so loud *they* literally woke me up! Then I knew I couldn't just lay there in bed any longer. I heard the words! I saw the words! By now, I'm all the way awake. After which, I heard in my spirit, "Get up and get your blessing."

What blessing? I thought.

It was early January, and it was very cold. Nonetheless, I got up. By now, in the midst of this, I was totally aware of my surroundings.

I should just mention, this kind of awakening was not unfamiliar to me. I had had those similar promptings before. But surely, I wasn't expecting one on this cold and early January morning! At this point, I believed the Lord was trying to get my attention. Then I wondered, what did He want me to do?

Therefore, I washed my face and went to my office in the adjacent room. From there it was almost instant that I had a strong urge to write. So I decided to sit in front of my computer and write about what you read next.

As I placed my fingers on the keyboard, I quickly wrote the words to the song that were constantly rolling over in my mind. It felt so right. I felt this was what the Holy Spirit was leading me to do. Then, my fingers began to move as if they were dancing swiftly across the keyboard. I found myself typing all the words that had penetrated my mind, as I had seen them through the fog: **ALL OF MY LIFE I'VE NEVER KNOWN YOU TO FAIL. YOU REMAIN THE SAME. WONDERFUL IS YOUR NAME!**

At this point, I was beginning to wonder if this was a dream or was it a vision from God? Could it be that God was showing me He was still in my midst, even after experiencing such a toilsome night before waking up that morning of January 2021?

Let me rewind by sharing what had occurred prior to that night. Upon getting into bed, I felt my life had come full circle in dealing with some challenges involving my loved one (previously mentioned), who had been struggling in a storm. At some point during that week, my loved one experienced some unexpected challenges. Realizing this, it was difficult for me to rest well that night. I was devastated that my loved one's struggle had gotten worse. I was tired and had become weary in being supportive time after time after time, trying to hold everything together.

I felt as if my loved one and I were back at point zero in dealing with this hardship, which was now seemingly turning into a crisis. I was at the point of overwhelming disappointment, hurt, and pain. I felt a sense of helplessness and hopelessness, accompanied by deep sorrow for my loved one, as well as myself.

From being made aware of my loved one's setback that week, I felt the crisis had won with no chance of recovery. Still, because of my trust and hope in God, I never ceased praying about that situation, at times having visions of God's miraculous intervention. Many times, it appeared as if God's healing was just on the horizon.

That said, on occasion, prior to the shutdown, I could sense the progress and positive change in my loved one. The improvement was evident. The storm appeared to be passing over. To all appearances, everything was getting better. My heart became hopeful again that God's intervention was imminent. But here it was again, that same storm appearing the first week of that New Year! I was devastated for my loved one and family to still be going through this seemingly unending battle!

For a moment, I struggled with, "Could all the hard work and prayers over the years been for nothing? Could my prayers be wasted because this crisis was now appearing worse than before?" I began to feel bad and miserable for my family and everyone who was affected by this critical time during the pandemic. I felt overwhelmed. And there it was—BAM! It hit me like a brick!

When I felt that BAM, I began to wrestle with God in prayer that night. I asked Him some serious questions before I finally fell asleep. My prayer went something like this:

> *Now, Lord, I find myself in a dilemma again. Do I continue to believe victory is going to take place? Do I give up on this situation, which seems to be happening over and over again, now appearing to get worse? Dear merciful God, I've been trusting You to take care of this situation, and You have shown me on many occasions (without a doubt) that You were right there. Help me to believe you're still here in the midst of this crisis! Show me that you are still working, Father. I thought You and I had such a beautiful relationship that I gained a great deal of confidence in You that You weren't going to allow the enemy to overtake my loved one nor me in the midst of this. But now, Lord, it seems You've removed your hand from us in the midst of this critical time of hurt and pain. Help me, O Lord, not to give up on You in this situation! Where are you, Lord?*

Yes, that was my prayer that night before I fell asleep. I know now that it was these kinds of thoughts and questions on that late night/early morning of January 10 that I allowed to creep in my bed with me, curl up under my covers, and rest in my bosom.

New Beginnings, Faith Up!

For me, it appeared as if all the hard work and progress to make that situation better had suddenly vanished and went down the drain. I also felt in that BAM moment all my strength was gone. I felt alone. Don't judge me, please. For I had unknowingly arrived in one of those BAM moments. I felt God had abandoned my family in the midst of this devastating struggle.

After which, all I thought to do was suck it up and try to convince myself to accept whatever comes. So as I lay down on my pillow that night, I thought, *Here I am, Lord, for all intents and purposes, back to the beginning of the onset of this crisis. Where do I go from here?*

I am ashamed to admit I was at the dangerous edge of doubting God despite all that He had brought my loved one and me through, such as the strength to prevail over the obstacles in this ongoing storm, the resources He had provided during the critical moments, and His constant care and protection during the worst times of the struggle. Still, I found I was on the verge of not trusting in the further guidance, protection, provision, and healing power of the God of the universe in the midst of *this* particular crisis.

Also, that night, as you might imagine, I was on the margin of being deeply disappointed in God that He had failed me during this critical time. Though I felt hopeless, I cried out in prayer before I finally fell asleep. But at five o'clock, as I slowly opened my eyes on that cold January morning, I literally saw in my dream through those aforementioned gigantic waves of letters clearly that God had not failed me. I sought Him and He answered.

He showed me He was fully aware of all my thoughts and that He saw how I had allowed the enemy to attack my mind. Still, God, in His love and faithfulness, came (actually, He never left). Therefore, I am so thankful that with His Word, He lifted the fog, calmed the waves of the sea, and rescued me so that I could see clearly: GOD NEVER FAILS. Realizing this, I needed to repent, and I did.

So on that faithful Sunday morning of January 10, 2021, I begged for the Lord to help me and forgive me for my under-sight of His grace and mercy. He did just that by reassuring me He still has my loved one's situation in His hand—and mine as well. He further assured me He's still in the midst of this!

He also brought to my mind Paul the Apostle, who lived with a thorn in his side and, after praying to the Lord three times to remove it, was told, "My grace is sufficient for you, for my power is made perfect in weakness" (2 Corinthians 12:9). I pray you are comforted and strengthened to know this applies to me and you and anyone who is still going through a struggle or hardship, crisis, or dilemma. His grace *is* sufficient. His power *is* made perfect in weakness.

It was then I began to understand that it's not about the thorn or the kind of storm at all! It's not about what we are going through as much as it is about *God's grace* to get us through. The focus is God's grace, not the thorn in Paul's side. Not the crisis my family is still going through. It's about God's grace and mercy. Knowing that His grace was sufficient in the midst of what Paul went through, it is also sufficient in what we are still going through. After being reminded of the power of God's grace, I prayed again: "Lord, I will still trust you in the midst of this, even if we have to start all over again. You have a purpose through it all."

And just as I had finished praying, I began sensing a new revelation in my spirit that I hadn't gone back to the beginning at all. With this crisis, I firmly believe God had allowed me to come to another starting point on another level of my faith in Him concerning this very same struggle. I only needed to faith up! I believe God was showing me each level of faith has new beginnings, new challenges, and possibly even some BAM moments. But don't fear. God is here.

So, in order to walk in this new level of faith, I was to gear up through believing prayer and FAITH UP on the platform God had brought me to in this struggle. I needed to be convinced God was still in the midst of this, even as we were still going through. And with this dream, my friends, He has done just that.

You may agree sometimes it can seem like starting over when things seem tougher, harder, more complicated—even lingering with no let up. But have you thought that you may not be starting over at all, but continuing to a higher knowledge of God by moving to another level of faith in Him? Consider what the apostles said to the Lord: "Increase our faith!" (Luke 17:5).

On that faithful morning, however, I'm happy to say that was not the end of my dream experience. To put the icing on this cake, that same morning, God gave me divine confirmation that He was aware of everything I was going through when I went to bed and during my sleep. As I shared before, I'm an adamant seeker of God's confirmation.

It so happened just as I had finished titling the previous segment "God Never Fails," I immediately went online to listen to my church's virtual worship that early morning. Would you believe, when I turned the computer on at that precise time, I heard a member and the choir singing words about the never-failing power of God! I remember saying in gratefulness, "Look at you, Lord!! Hallelujah!" I heard words that reflected how great our God is and hailed Him as our Conqueror and our Deliverer and reminded me that He's never failed, even through trials and tribulations can appear insurmountable.

I'm aware some may say this timing was a coincidence, but I say it was providence. I believe it was God still comforting, strengthening, and assuring me what to do while I was still going through by way of a dream and now by providing His confirmation through actual virtual worship that same morning.

Therefore, I say *HALLELUJAH* to the prompting of the Holy Spirit at 5:00 a.m. that morning on January 10, 2021, to "get up, gear up, and get my blessing"! And what a blessing I received to be reminded and encouraged through what I now believe was a vision instead of a dream, that God is still the all-unfailing God, and He will never fail me, no matter the struggle or length thereof.

I'm even more confident He is still working in the struggles my family and my loved one are still facing, just as He has been from the beginning. I say thank You, Lord, for coming to my rescue at the dawn of that day. Thank You for refreshing my memory, strengthening and comforting my heart, in the midst of this, in the knowledge of You to faith up! For surely, You are God who never fails.

In the Midst of This, Gear Up in the Knowledge of God

For my thoughts are not your thoughts, neither are your ways my ways, declares the LORD. *For as the heavens are higher than the earth, so are my ways higher than your ways and my thoughts than your thoughts.*

—Isaiah 55: 8–9

But grow in the grace and knowledge of our Lord and Savior Jesus Christ. To him be the glory both now and to the day of eternity. Amen.

—2 Peter 3:18

I do not cease to give thanks for you, remembering you in my prayers, that the God of our Lord Jesus Christ, the Father of glory, may give you the Spirit of wisdom and of revelation in the knowledge of him.

—Ephesians 1:16–17

CHAPTER 6

Gear Up in Faith and Trust

A re you aware the knowledge of God helps us to gear up in both our faith and trust in Him? I paired these two together because I find it difficult to have one without the other. To have one produces action from the other. To gear up in one is to gear up with the other.

Can we actually say, "I have faith in God, but I don't trust God?" Will that be good enough for Him? Would that be pleasing to Him? For me, that's like saying, "I have faith to believe God is who He says He is, but I don't trust Him to do what He says He can do." Strictly speaking, the more we know about God in His Word, the more faith we gain that He can be trusted.

One thing is for sure, when we have faith and trust in God, we are bound to worry less about the stresses that could come our way. If we are honest, we worry needlessly. Certainly, it can be hard for us not to worry when we think there's nothing we can do about a very challenging and stressful situation. I'm reminded of the time when Jesus and His disciples were on a boat in the midst of a violent storm, as Jesus was asleep, and the waves overflowed into the boat (Matt. 8:23–27). The disciples feared for their lives. Finally, they woke up Jesus and said to Him, "Save us, Lord; we are perishing." Jesus' reply to them was, "Why are you afraid, O you of little faith?" Despite their fears, and I imagine extreme worry, Jesus "arose and rebuked the winds and the sea and there was a great calm." Here's a thought: Knowing Jesus has the power to calm the waves of the sea, how much more can He calm in you and me if we put all our trust and faith in Him?

It's definitely easy to worry when we don't possess the faith to believe that God can handle all our worries and fears. Trust that God wants to strengthen our faith and build our trust in Him. I'm simply saying if we're staying awake worrying all night long, something is terribly wrong with our faith and trust in Him. Why not say to yourself, *In the midst of this, I won't worry about it. I will trust in God.* And, of course, this can be easier said than done. Yet it can be done.

Faith calls for belief without doubting God has our situation in His hand. It means putting our confidence in Him that He will fulfill His promises. Therefore, having faith should increase our trust in God. When this is done, our entire being will not be anxious because we have gained the assurance that lets us know God will help us in times of need.

I'm convinced faith and trust work mighty good together while going through difficult moments. They help us to remain steadfast in God, regardless of how long our trials last. Not only that, but they encourage us God is in the midst of our struggles to bring His will to pass. So if we would rest in Him and listen to His voice, we can get through without being overcome by worrying. Let me draw your attention to a simple short story of a prayer warrior as opposed to a worrier.

Warrior or Worrier—A Confirmation of Faith

Once upon a time, there was a God-fearing warrior who thought she had learned to let go and let God handle all her worries and cares. One night, after finally making a tough decision about an intense matter, she went to bed and fell peacefully asleep. Then, around 3:45 a.m., she woke up and began wondering if she had made the right decision. And that was okay. But what wasn't okay was when she began worrying about the possibility of negative outcomes as a result of the decision she had made.

In her mind, she went from one undesirable outcome to the next. After realizing she was caught up with the negative outcomes, the God-fearing warrior began to notice she was getting a bit anxious, restless, and couldn't go back to sleep.

Becoming aware of her thought pattern, she recognized this kind of damaging thinking could only be coming from one source, her old archenemy, Ole Lady Worry. To her surprise, the God-fearing warrior had allowed Ole Lady Worry to sneak into her mind.

You may ask, how did the God-fearing warrior know it was Ole Lady Worry? She knew it was her because their paths had crossed before. Ole Lady Worry had tried to overtake the God-fearing warrior more than once. Now, the God-fearing warrior knew she had only returned to try it again. And because of the God-fearing warrior's faith and knowledge of God's

Word, she remembered what weapon was needed to combat Ole Lady Worry.

In the past, when the God-fearing warrior began to be restless, she would gear up in her faith with her weapon of prayer. She knew in her distress that her God had always been there to answer her. He would always come to her rescue. By faith, she had no doubt He would do it again.

Being that the God-fearing warrior remembered how she finally overcame Ole Lady Worry through past encounters, she made it a practice to never be without her weapon. She kept it in her heart. She never left home or slept without it. It became her shield of protection even while she was sleeping. She had only to draw on it.

Through her prior experiences with Ole Lady Worry, the God-fearing warrior found that when she chose to use her weapon of prayer in faith, Ole Lady Worry had to step aside no matter how elegantly she was dressed, high heels and all!

So you'll know, prayer was the only thing Ole Lady Worry couldn't stand. She couldn't bear the voice of prayer. You understand Ole Lady Worry and the voice of believing prayer were no friends. They simply couldn't abide together. Because of the God-fearing warrior's faith in her God, she knew prayer was the answer to annihilate Ole Lady Worry.

With that said, unfortunately, worriers tend to lie down and wallow in their fears and anxieties, whereas God-fearing warriors choose to call on the God of War in the midst of what they're going through. As you can guess, that was all the God-fearing warrior needed to do, and she did it.

When she started praying, her peaceful sleep returned. You may ask, what ever happened to Ole Lady Worry? Oh, I don't know. All I can tell you is she did what she always does when she meets the Word of faith in prayer—Ole Lady Worry goes away!

In the Midst of This, Gear Up in Faith

For we walk by faith, not by sight.
—2 Corinthians 5:7

Now faith is the assurance of things hoped for, the conviction of things not seen.
—Hebrews 11:1

He said to them, "Because of your little faith. For truly, I say to you, if you have faith like a grain of mustard seed, you will say to this mountain, 'Move from here to there,' and it will move, and nothing will be impossible for you."
—Matthew 17:20

Through a Whisper—A Confirmation to Trust

Trust in the Lord. Most people who know me know I've shared that this statement has followed and comforted me all during my early move to California. After a few years of marriage, my husband and I joined a little local church in our community in LA. It was a Bible-toting, Bible-reading, and teaching church. I had never heard God's Word expounded like I had witnessed from the minister of that little church located on a very busy street corner in Los Angeles.

That minister, who became my pastor during the early years of my marriage, eventually passed away after pastoring for many years. Prior to his passing, he admonished my husband and me to memorize a particular scripture and to teach it to our children. That was his method for us to remember God's Word and to keep it in our hearts.

It seemed we were always memorizing and learning scriptures in that little church. Sometimes, the pastor would teach on one scripture for weeks on end. I learned to appreciate the many revelations and applications that could come forth from meditating on just *one* scripture—other times, just *one word*.

The scripture he encouraged us to learn and to teach our children was: "Trust in the Lord with all thine heart and lean not unto thine own understanding. In all thy ways acknowledge him and He shall direct thy paths. Be not wise in thine own eyes: fear the LORD, and depart from evil" (Proverbs 3:5-7, KJV). Yes, that was the scripture for us to live by! Somehow, God has a way of bringing this scripture to the forefront of my life at the most difficult moments as a reminder He's still with me.

Over the years, I cannot tell you the many times we had to turn to God by using this scripture while seeking His guidance, strength, and confirmation to press on. Although that was many years ago when I was first introduced to this scripture, it's still a source of comfort and strength for me today—to trust in the Lord with all my heart and lean not unto my own understanding.

Fast forward to present day. On one occasion, my current pastor encouraged us to memorize this scripture for our memory verse for a particular week. I praised God for that. Even though I was already familiar with the scripture (years back), I felt in my own life it was coming up again for a reason. So I began praying that scripture right away.

It so happened at this particular time our family was still continuing to battle in that same struggle our loved one was going through. When the struggle first came to light, that scripture immediately popped into my mind as an encouragement to keep holding on to my trust in God.

Have you ever had one of those moments where God's Word seemed to be right before your very eyes, even when everything seemed to be going topsy-turvy? Well, during that time, it appeared like the only thing God left me to do during that struggle was to pray and hold on to Proverbs 3:5–7, believing He would work it out.

As in times before, I began again seeking confirmation from Him as to what He wanted me to do while we were continuing in this family struggle. Here's the way God strengthened me on what to do by using this same scripture (Proverbs 3:5–7). It began with a still, small voice, as of a whisper. This was confirmed to me in four ways at four different times in one day as I continued to cry out to Him for an answer.

First, in my spirit one early morning, I heard like a whisper, "Just trust Me." I began meditating on that whisper throughout that morning. Next, I heard through the memory verse given by our pastor for that week to trust in the Lord (as mentioned). I continued praying on this scripture as the day went on.

Following that, this same scripture was the main focus of a lesson I was listening to on my television after church that early afternoon. The title of the lesson was to trust in the Lord. The television evangelist quoted the scripture and expounded on it as if he were speaking directly to me. Indeed, now God had my attention.

And finally, later that same day, while I was exercising to some gospel music, I heard a verse from a singer singing it: "Trust in the Lord with all your heart." I can't express to you the joy I experienced in that moment after hearing this verse throughout the same day at four different intervals. I was convinced God was confirming that the whisper I had heard that early morning was indeed His message of trust to me.

I knew then, without a shadow of a doubt, that hearing this same scripture four different times during that day was a sure confirmation that God was calling me to trust Him again and not to worry about the struggle we were still facing. I'm learning God can put His Word right in the midst of a situation to give his children assurance, hope, comfort, peace, and confirmation to clear away any doubt that He has the situation covered. And yes, for me that day, it began with a whisper.

In the Midst of This, Gear Up in Trust

And after the earthquake a fire, but the LORD was not in the fire. And after the fire the sound of a low whisper. And when Elijah heard it, he wrapped his face in his cloak and went out and stood at the entrance of the cave. And behold, there came a voice to him and said, "What are you doing here, Elijah?"

—1 Kings 19:12–13

Let me hear in the morning of your steadfast love, for in you I trust. Make me know the way I should go, for to you I lift up my soul.

—Psalm 143:8

You keep him in perfect peace whose mind is stayed on you, because he trusts in you.

—Isaiah 26:3

CHAPTER 7

Gear Up in Patience

ometimes we get in a hurry, don't we? And sometimes, we want God to act in the moment to help us. Then, sometimes, *we* want to act in that moment as well. Often enough, many of us try to help God fix our situation. I'm pretty sure I can get everyone to agree on this statement—none of us want to remain in a challenging, lingering situation.

On the other hand, no one wants something disastrous to pop up in their lives all of a sudden. Unfortunately, if it does, we would like it to be resolved as quickly as it came. By desiring that, we tend to try to fix it ourselves first without calling on God for direction. I hope you know when we're going through something, if we are patient, we could get to see God's hand at work.

Understandably, many times, challenging moments cannot be avoided. Some may come to test us. Still, we ask, what do we do when they happen? Do we cry and wallow in self-pity? As many of us have experienced, this approach does not work. It is not a viable solution. It could leave us with persistent headaches and heartaches, not to mention possibly swollen and red eyes, causing some to wear sunglasses in the shade. Well, in the midst of this, what do we do while we're still going through?

Now I say to you, not only do we gear up in faith and trust, but also in patience. We gear up by learning to wait in a godly way. Here's a definition of patience that got my attention: "Patience is the capacity to accept or tolerate delay, trouble, or suffering without 'acting' in anger or upset-ness."[1] That said, once we *act*, patience is no longer activated or demonstrated. But when we have come to the point of not acting in anger or upset-ness, godly patience has taken place in our hearts. We can rest and believe that when patience comes, we can be calm.

We understand patience doesn't automatically happen. We can't click our heels, snap our fingers, or wish upon a star for patience. We pray to God for it. God's Word encourages us to "rejoice in hope, be patient in tribulation, be constant in prayer" (Romans 12:12). Also, in Romans 5:3-4 we read, "Not only that, but we rejoice in our sufferings, knowing that suffering produces endurance, and endurance produces character, and character produces hope."

With these scriptures, I was reminded of the patience of Job, who God allowed to be tested. I thought of how Job persevered in the face of longsuffering. It appeared as if *stuff* just started popping up in Jobs's life, one tragedy after the next. But He

---

[1] "Patience," *Dictionary.com*.

waited and endured, though God allowed the enemy to finally strike him with sores. As he endured, he prayed and was even patient enough through his suffering to hear the blows and cons from his friends. Now, that requires a lot of patience, wouldn't you say?

Not only Job, but there were others in the Bible that the Bible didn't mention specifically about their patience in suffering, but nevertheless, they went through long ordeals with suffering in one way or the other. There was the woman with the issue of blood who suffered for twelve long years. When she encountered Jesus, she was healed (Mark 5). The Bible also tells of a man who was paralyzed for thirty-eight years and was restored physically (John 5). What's more, the Bible informs of a boy born blind from birth, and Jesus restored his sight (John 9). We remember Paul (as mentioned earlier), who had a thorn in his side. Jesus' response to him was His grace is sufficient, and His power is made perfect in weakness.

By reading biblical accounts like these, some may wonder if this suggests to gain patience, there will be some suffering and long waits. Well, quite possibly, but not necessarily so to this magnitude. We who trust God learn to wait in patience despite it all. By having patience, we learn to endure. With endurance, we can encourage others to trust God as they are still going through difficult times.

As we continue to gear up in patience, we will come to learn that difficult times do not always come to work against us but to help us. How we respond when they do come is the question.

Here's a thought: Could it be that God is allowing us to be in that moment to give us something we've been praying for all along—some good ole godly patience? Be confident that godly patience is another principle that will provide us the strength to endure while the storm is still going on in our lives.

In the Midst of This, Gear Up in Patience

But if we hope for what we do not see, we wait for it with patience.

—Romans 8:25

You also, be patient. Establish your hearts, for the coming of the Lord is at hand.

—James 5:8

Wait for the LORD; be strong, and let your heart take courage; wait for the LORD!

—Psalm 27:14

CHAPTER 8

Gear Up in Hope

L et me begin by saying life can bring us down if we let it. Life can sap all the energy out of us if we allow it. The trials we go through. The setbacks we didn't expect. The raise we didn't get. That divorce. The grief of a loved one's passing. A wayward child. A struggling marriage. A sudden tragedy. All these and more can bring on despair if we don't possess the next principle, which is a godly hope.

This is the kind of hope that helps us to maintain regardless of our pain. The only hope that can do this is the hope we find in Christ. To possess this hope is to have the confident affirmation that God is faithful and that He will complete what He has begun, no matter what we go through.

By now, I *hope* you are becoming aware that *In the Midst of This* is endeavoring to provide godly truths that will help you remain steadfast in your hope in God. Having your hope saturated in Christ gives you a better insight on the trials you may face on your journey. As stated, *endurance (meaning patience) produces character, and character produces hope.* Also, by this, as we endure the hardships of life, we are being strengthened through them and building a secure hope in Christ.

Let me be clear: Hope for the Christian does not mean simply wishing upon a star. When I think of wishing, I sometimes think I could be disappointed. Simply because if I didn't get what I wished for, I could feel let down. But the hope I have in Christ will never disappoint me. It will never let me down. It pumps me up. It provides me with a reason to live. It gives me something to look forward to. It is lasting and enduring to help me get through the tough times of life.

Accordingly, the hope we have in Christ provides us with a sound focus on a definite, everlasting future with Christ. As one scripture (Jeremiah 29:11) encourages us, "For I know the plans I have for you, declares the LORD, plans for welfare and not for evil, to give you a future and a hope." So no, this kind of hope does not come by far by wishing upon a star. It comes from God Himself.

He is faithful to His Word. He is faithful to the plans He has for us. And yes, sometimes, within these plans, we can find ourselves going through tough challenges. But don't give up. Hold on to hope. This means to be steadfast in our confidence so we won't lose hope.

With hope, we maintain a confident expectation that God is there to keep us from falling into despair. Don't lose heart. He's also there to keep us from falling apart. Hence, to gear up in hope is to gear up in utter assurance of God's Word that He is faithful.

Furthermore, Romans 5:5 leaves us with a promise: "And hope does not put us to shame, because God's love has been poured into our hearts through the Holy Spirit who has been given to us." What a blessing to know we will not be made ashamed when we place our hope in God. I don't believe anyone can say they were made ashamed by putting their hope in God.

You may ask, so how do I gear up in this hope? The answer is very clear. Stay focused on the God of hope. What do I mean by that? Focus on His very character, His nature, His love, His faithfulness. As the Bible informs us, it is His love that has been poured into our hearts through the Holy Spirit that was given to us. His love for us gives us hope that everything we go through is not for nothing. It's not in vain.

So let us keep on focusing on the voice of God when times seem hopeless. Paying attention to His voice helps us to gear up in hope. Listening to and obeying His voice will get us through the hard trials of life. Thus, we should be still in the midst of our struggles so that we can hear His voice. Sometimes, His voice is so very still. He speaks all the more.

When He speaks, I pray we don't miss it but are encouraged that while we are still going through, God, by way of the Holy Spirit, is with us to talk to us. "He who has ears to hear, let him hear" (Matthew 11:15). Simply pause, get still, and listen. We just might hear Him admonishing us not to give up but to hold on a little while longer—holding on to the hope we have in Him.

In contrast, I hope you are aware there are also voices trying to bring us down in despair. These voices will try to get us to believe things have gotten so bad that there is no hope left. This is why it's so important to gear up by staying in the Word of God, which gives us hope. By doing this, we will be able to distinguish which voice to listen to.

By gearing up in God's Word, we come to know His Word gives us hope not only for today but also for tomorrow. I pray we trust that the same God who brought us through today is beyond capable of bringing us through tomorrow. The Bible reminds us, "Therefore do not be anxious about tomorrow, for tomorrow will be anxious for itself. Sufficient for the day is its own trouble" (Matthew 6:34).

Since there is so much good news in God's Word, I pray you gear up so you will be confident in where your hope lies. That confidence comes by believing in the power of God and that He is faithful to keep you while you are still struggling.

Truly it is God who helps us to lift our minds in the darkest of the day and in the longest of the night. He is the one to help us see our way through these trying times. Even when we don't see the light at the end of the tunnel, or amidst the cloudy sky, we maintain hope that there is one because of who God is. His light is evident to those who have faith that He is faithful. I pray you experience the light of God's grace shining over your life as you may be still going through.

I pray we also trust that as long as we can hold on to the God of hope, we have a good grip. He has never dropped anyone, and He will not drop you nor me. I cannot say it enough—rest in God and put all your hope in Him.

In the Midst of This, Gear Up in Hope

Why are you cast down, O my soul, and why are you in turmoil within me? Hope in God; for I shall again praise him, my salvation and my God.
—Psalm 42:5

May the God of hope fill you with all joy and peace in believing, so that by the power of the Holy Spirit you may abound in hope.
—Romans 15:13

Blessed be the God and Father of our Lord Jesus Christ! According to his great mercy, he has caused us to be born again to a living hope through the resurrection of Jesus Christ from the dead.
—1 Peter 1:3

69

CHAPTER 9

Gear Up in Strength

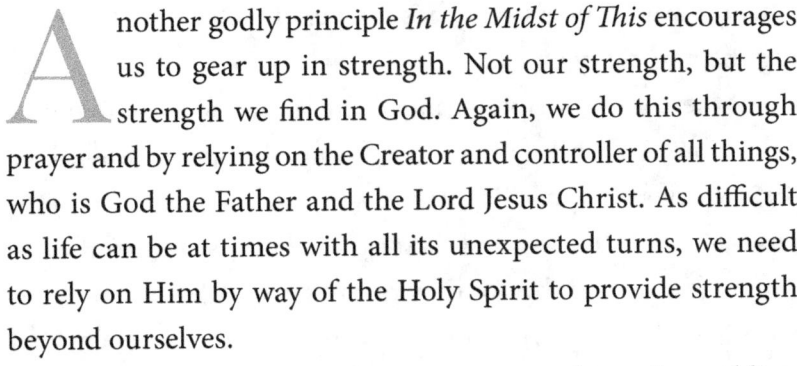

A nother godly principle *In the Midst of This* encourages us to gear up in strength. Not our strength, but the strength we find in God. Again, we do this through prayer and by relying on the Creator and controller of all things, who is God the Father and the Lord Jesus Christ. As difficult as life can be at times with all its unexpected turns, we need to rely on Him by way of the Holy Spirit to provide strength beyond ourselves.

It's been proven time after time—to get through troubling moments, strength is very much needed, whether it is emotional strength, physical strength, spiritual strength, social, domestic, mental or financial strength. One thing is for certain, we don't have the power in and of ourselves to surmount these troubling times alone.

Certainly, the world has seen and experienced many things in its time, especially with the worldwide pandemic. Yet it is still standing. All praises be to God! Where, you may ask, do people get their strength from to withstand and persevere during some of these most trying of times?

May I submit to you: The only name I know that I have come to rely on and depend on in the midst of all I've been through is the name of Jesus. I can affirm and attest He is my strength. He is the One who teaches me to gear up in the midst of insurmountable circumstances.

Since we, by God's grace, have made it alive through COVID-19, I pray we're gearing ourselves up more to draw on His strength. Although, as a result of the pandemic, many still find themselves being stretched beyond measure by dealing with situation after situation, change after change, I hope they can attest that God's strength is still very much evident in helping them to carry on.

If there is one scripture many Christians have laid to memory before and while going through hardships, it is Philippians 4:13, which says, "I can do all things through him who strengthens me." We often rely on this scripture because it is confirmation we are not on this journey by ourselves. We are not alone. God is with us to strengthen us. It makes no difference what God uses and how He chooses to strengthen us; we should rest in the fact that He is the one who does it.

Just saying, in the midst of a physical illness, a doctor can prescribe the medicine to be taken but cannot provide the strength to get better. An exercise coach can lay out a wonderful workout regime but cannot make us stronger. To get the benefit and be strengthened in situations like these, we must put in the required work.

In the spiritual sense, however, we can gear up in strength through God's Word. Now, that will work. The question is, again, how do we do this while we're still going through? The answer is not that vague. For us to gear up in strength, we must *keep on relying* on the Strengthener, who is Christ Jesus.

We should put all our trust and faith in Him by going daily to His spiritual pharmacy to pick up His prescription for strength. You may have guessed by now—His spiritual pharmacy is His Holy Bible, the Word of God. There lies the prescription written that is needed to get us through.

In light of that, what is God's prescription for strength? Himself, according to His Word. It can't get any clearer than that. Psalm 46:1 tells us, "God is our refuge and strength, a very present help in trouble." He will strengthen you and show you what needs to be done. Yes, He alone is the Strengthener in every case and in every way through the power of the Holy Spirit.

I don't want anyone who is reading this book to think for a moment that they are strong enough by themselves to endure the storms of life. I want you to rest in the fact that Christ has made His strength available in the midst of your *this* for you to get through *it*. Also, according to this above scripture, allow me to encourage you further by shining the light on the kind of strengthener we have in Christ.

We have a strengthener who is a *very present* help in times of trouble. Meaning, He's not absent from our troubles, regardless of how long they last. He's not *just* present. He's *very* present. He's right there in the midst, and He's not in the midst for nothing. As the scripture reminds us, He's in the midst to help us. To offer His divine service.

Besides that, He's also a strengthener who will advise us while we're still going through. As I forementioned, His name is Jesus. If only we make ready through His Word, we will be able to gain strength to prevail much better while the struggle is still going on in our lives.

In the Midst of This, Gear Up in Strength

He gives power to the faint, and to him who has no might he increases strength.

—Isaiah 40:29

Seek the LORD and his strength; seek his presence continually!

—1 Chronicles 16:11

That according to the riches of his glory he may grant you to be strengthened with power through his Spirit in your inner being, so that Christ may dwell in your hearts through faith—that you, being rooted and grounded in love.

—Ephesians 3:16–17

CHAPTER 10

Gear Up in Gratefulness

W ell, this is where we have arrived—to the beautiful subject of gratefulness. Gratefulness is a warm and deep appreciation for kindness received, gratitude, or thankfulness. I'm willing to bet we all have felt this wonderful feeling of being thankful or receiving an acknowledgment of thanks. It can be so satisfying to the giver as well as the receiver.

Sure enough, expressing gratitude can help lift our minds away from what may be causing discomfort in our lives to the good that can come forth. Although we do not know what a day may bring, waking up with a grateful heart should give us a better start and outlook. In addition, expressing gratefulness can help us to get a clearer picture of our blessings. Therefore, I pray we gear up in our appreciation to God for His lovingkindness toward us every day.

I imagine you already know that every morning we wake up is an expression of God's great love for us. Every morning we're able to get up is another declaration of His great love. Also, every morning we can move anything is indeed a pronouncement of His great love for us. Remember God is love, and He shows His love to us even when we don't show love back to Him. For this reason, being gifted with His love, surely we have something to be thankful for.

Here are more reasons that should cause us to gear up in gratefulness to God. He alone is the reason we can feel, see, live, move, or do anything. "For 'in him we live and move and have our being'; as even some of your poets have said, 'For we are indeed his offspring'" (Acts 17:28). From this scripture, we understand it's only because of Christ that we have life.

This brings to mind that to gear up in gratefulness is to always thank and acknowledge God for who He is. I encourage you to read more of God's Word so you will discover *who* you are really thanking. For one thing, according to this scripture, we will find that He is the Giver and Sustainer of life. He is the very cause of our existence. That being, He deserves to be honored from a grateful heart.

Do you know expressing gratefulness to God is not a light thing? It is huge. Are you aware God takes pleasure in us maintaining a grateful heart toward Him, even while we are going through some of the worst times of our lives? How do you express your gratitude when going through difficult times? Do you forget about God? Or do you express to Him you are still thankful for His care?

In the Midst of This

Another way to gear up in gratefulness is to make a conscious effort and habit of expressing thankfulness and appreciation to God for every facet of our lives, even when we don't understand why things are happening as they do. Be thankful in the bad times as well as the good times. The Bible tells us to "give thanks in all circumstances, for this is the will of God in Christ Jesus for you" (1 Thessalonians 5:18). So, if we are expressing gratefulness, we tend to be thankful before, during, and after difficult situations occur in our lives. We will not be so quick to throw our hands up in the air in despair. Why not look for something to be thankful for in the midst of what we are facing in order to maintain an attitude of gratitude.

Another way to gear up in gratefulness is by gearing up not only with what our mouth proclaims but by manifesting God-honoring actions. When we say, "Lord, I thank you," that is always a good start. By saying thank you, we have struck the match (so to speak). But when we act in gratefulness, the match is lit. And when that match is lit, our expression and appreciation to God is manifested by a burning desire to *do* something more.

Have you considered *saying* "I thank you" and *expressing* "I thank you" are different? Of course, both are acceptable and glorifying to God when coming from a sincere heart of gratitude. However, one is an acknowledgment, and the other is an action. *Saying* "I thank you" is an acknowledgment. *Expressing*

"I thank you" is an action. Many times, when we've geared up in gratefulness, an action will follow the acknowledgment.

For example, one way our action of worship follows our acknowledgment of worship is by actually *worshipping God.* Worship is an action and is a God-honoring expression of gratefulness to Him. Worshipping God for who He is displays action. This demonstrates our deep appreciation and adoration for and to Him.

We also express our gratefulness by praising Him and doing for others, helping others, and giving to others. With that, are you grateful that you can do for others since you are aware of how much God has done for you? Because of who God is, what God has done, *and* what He has done in *our* lives, I hope we gear up to not only say, "Lord, I'm thankful," but express with a grateful heart, "Lord, I'm thankful." I hope your prayer goes somewhat like this:

> *Dear Lord. Thank you. You have done so much for me that I must say, in the midst of this, I praise you!*
>
> *I'm thankful for your wonderful grace and mercy toward me; Therefore, Lord, I lift my hands to you.*
>
> *I'm thankful for what you did back on Calvary. Therefore, Lord, I worship and adore you.*

I'm thankful for the knowledge of your Word.
Therefore, Lord, I appreciate you.

I'm thankful for you providing for me. Therefore,
Lord, I gladly do for others.

Based on what you've read, I pray you have a more grateful heart toward God when viewing your circumstances. I hope you have come to realize things are not as bad as they could be. By your eyes becoming open to this, I pray by now your heart is geared with gratefulness.

Furthermore, when we gear up in gratefulness, we acknowledge our total dependency on God for everything. We give Him thanks for being *who* we need every day and *who* we need in the midst of our trials. He is the Father of mercies and the God of all comfort. He is our source of strength, blessings, and power. So why not thank Him for providing the gear that is necessary to get through another day?

For sure, what we practice becomes a part of us. I encourage you to practice gratefulness in the midst of what you're still going through every day. Here's a simple prayer to encourage you as you go through.

Lord, I thank You, In the Midst of This:

For being my Anchor, Blesser, Comfort, Director,
Enlightener, and Friend.

Thank You for being my Guide, Hope, Inspirer, Joy, Keeper, and Lifter, now and to the end.

Thank You for being my Might, Nurturer, Operator, Peace, Quieter, Refuge, Soother, and Trust.

Upholder, Victor, Watcher, X-ray of Life, Yoke Releaser, and Zeal,

For me and all of us.

In the Midst of This, Gear Up in Gratefulness

For it is all for your sake, so that as grace extends to more and more people it may increase thanksgiving, to the glory of God.
—2 Corinthians 4:15

I will give thanks to the LORD with my whole heart; I will recount all of your wonderful deeds.
—Psalm 9:1

Offer to God a sacrifice of thanksgiving, and perform your vows to the Most High, and call upon me in the day of trouble; I will deliver you, and you shall glorify me.
—Psalm 50:14–15

CHAPTER 11

Gear Up in Your Outlook

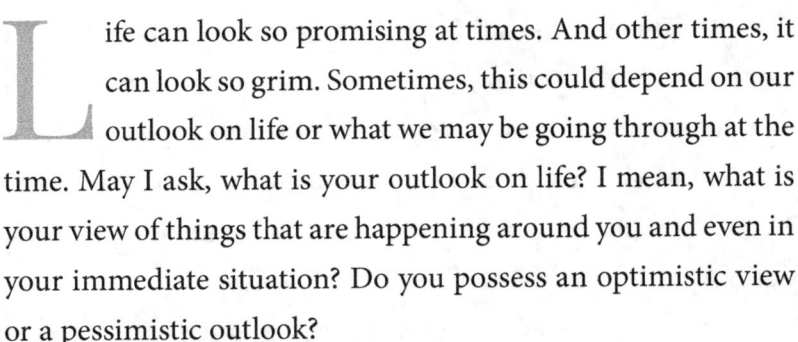

L ife can look so promising at times. And other times, it can look so grim. Sometimes, this could depend on our outlook on life or what we may be going through at the time. May I ask, what is your outlook on life? I mean, what is your view of things that are happening around you and even in your immediate situation? Do you possess an optimistic view or a pessimistic outlook?

I hope you are a firm believer that how we view life could determine if we make it or be broken by it. How we perceive our situation can affect whether we will press through or not. Unfortunately, if we keep looking down at our situations and not upward toward God, a lot of us will fail to see ourselves pressing through. As you might imagine, this kind of outlook tends to make it so hard to stay positive and hopeful.

I understand as bad as things sometimes seem to be, it can be difficult to maintain a positive attitude. Yet and still, because of these uncertain and challenging times, I suggest we gear up in our outlook because there is no benefit in looking hopeless in life. Especially for those of us who say we know Christ. Again, we do this by equipping ourselves through prayer and reading God's Word. This is sure to give a better perspective on our situation and the future.

So despite what is happening in the world, please know our eternal future is secure in God if we have accepted Jesus as our personal Savior. For certain, if we are reading our Bible, we should not be surprised as to the current state of our world affairs. The Bible alerts us that these evil and troubling times will come. It also tells us that Jesus said, "I have said these things to you, that in me you may have peace. In the world you will have tribulation. But take heart; I have overcome the world" (John 16:33). As such, we should pray to continue with an optimistic outlook in life.

Just to say, the way we view what is happening can make the difference in a restful night's sleep or a sleepless night, holding on or giving up, and staying sane or going insane. So whether we succeed or not will depend on *how* we look at the things that happen to us. Our outlook on things can be just that serious.

A person once shared with me, "Many times, if we don't have a positive outlook, we might look at the difficult things in our lives as a penalty for something we may have done or are not doing." She went on to share, "This is not always the case. We should look to the *purpose* instead of a penalty."

From her statement, I'm confident that considering God's purpose is a far better outlook than feelings of being punished. For this reason, I hope we learn to gear up in our spiritual outlook by realizing that God has a divine purpose and deeper meaning from the many experiences we go through in our lives. Also, that He has our life in His hand.

By her words, I thought of these scriptures, "And we know that for those who love God all things work together for good, for those who are called according to his purpose" (Romans 8:28). Also, Ephesians 1:11 states, "In him we have obtained an inheritance, having been predestined according to the purpose of him who works all things according to the counsel of his will." On remembering this, I was more encouraged that God has a divine purpose for my life, and He has not left me alone to figure things out, though sometimes many of us try.

Nevertheless, when we look to Jesus in prayer beforehand, we will gain a better understanding as to the strange and unpredictable happenings in our lives. They are not all meant for bad or to kill us. I am still holding to the argument that whatever we may still be encountering, it's not up to us to handle it on our own. I urge you to first seek God for insight on how to proceed while facing hardships.

When we ask God how to proceed, He is faithful to reveal ways to help us to continue. Sometimes, the pain and hurt can be so deep all we want to do is cry. But as many of us have experienced, crying is not going to solve the problems (as shared earlier). And yes, sometimes crying does provide a temporary relief. But it won't change the situation.

So if you are one of those who think by crying long enough, your troubles will go away, you may be losing in your struggle. On the other hand, you may think all you need to do is stop crying, suck it up, and ignore it altogether. No, that's not the answer either. To suck it up could be like burying your troubles in a very shallow grave while you are still carrying the weight of it. I can say this because it has happened to me (Chapter 5). I imagine many others have experienced this as well. I found out it is best to call on and look to Jesus for help to face any troubles, concerns, and misfortunes instead of trying to carry them in unhealthy ways without Him. Although we sometimes fall, Jesus is always there to pick us up.

I'm fully aware there are those who have not accepted Jesus as their personal Savior. As a result, they do not look to Him in the midst of their circumstances, and yet it appears they are getting through without seeking His help. You may ask why does this happen? For one thing, God's mercy and grace still ring loud for the unsaved as they do for the saved. Remember, God rains on the just as well as the unjust and is long-suffering toward all. He is no respecter of persons.

Moreover, be confident in this: As believers, we have a Savior we can take all our burdens to. We don't have to bear them in our own strength in the midst of difficult times, as do the unsaved. We are free to cast our troubles to the Lord in believing prayer. For He said in His Word, "Come to me, all who labor and are heavy laden, and I will give you rest" (Matthew 11:28). This promise is only to the ones who will come. If you are unsaved, Jesus is welcoming you right now to come unto Him and be saved.

Also, be assured God is not going to allow anyone to interfere or stop His plan, program, or purpose. He has the final *Word*. And lastly, His purpose is greater than any of us—believer or unbeliever.

I still maintain that if we are still going through, we need God's help. When we focus our sight on Him, no doubt He will show us what we need. Are you aware He will show us even if it requires seeking professional help? Do not be afraid or ashamed to get professional help if you are in a medical or mental crisis, if need be.

Know God is so good and wise in His care for us that He has set medical professionals in place. He has set them in place, not only for the secular world but also for we who seek Him. He is just that rich in wisdom. He is the only one who knows how to direct us in the midst of what we're still going through to the help that He has made available.

By now, I hope you realize gearing up with a good outlook by looking to Jesus is essential to whether we stand or fall, whether we keep on stumbling over the same thing or stay the course. Thus, keeping our focus on God provides us with the insight of knowing God is always in control. With Him being our forerunner, guide, support, encourager, and sustainer, we are able to face and press through the hard times in life. I hope, *In the Midst of This*, you come to the same conclusion.

In the Midst of This, Gear Up in your Outlook

Set your minds on things that are above, not on things that are on earth.

—Colossians 3:2

I lift up my eyes to the hills. From where does my help come? My help comes from the LORD, who made heaven and earth.

—Psalm 121:1–2

Therefore, since we are surrounded by so great a cloud of witnesses, let us also lay aside every weight and sin which clings so closely, and let us run with endurance the race that is set before us, looking to Jesus, the founder and perfecter of our faith, who for the joy that was set before him endured the cross, despising the shame, and is seated at the right hand of the throne of God.

—Hebrews 12:1–2

Food for Thought

After reading *In the Midst of This*, I hope one of your main takeaways will be God is in the midst of whatever you're going through, and He's able to sustain and keep you through it all. I hope you realize He has blessed us in His Word with spiritual principles to help us gear up before and sometimes during difficult and tragic moments. Please be confident: He is with us to bring light, purpose, revelation, strength, comfort, hope, and focus to our circumstances.

Also, according to His Word, He has promised through sorrow, grief, pain, loneliness, and brokenness, He will never leave or forsake us. I pray you believe Him. His Word tells us He is nearer to us than when we first believed. So it doesn't matter how difficult or cloudy it looks or is—know that God is here. He is here by way of the Holy Spirit to bring us to a place of new revelation and peace in Him.

When we're at this place of peace, our mindset will change. It will be changed from focusing much on ourselves and our problems (as if we are all alone to handle them). Instead, our minds will be focused on the power of the Almighty God and His faithfulness in the midst of what we're going through.

Truly, when we think like this, we will not be consumed by

what has happened to us but that God is in charge. He knows what He is doing in our lives. We must learn to trust Him. When it comes clear, then we should pray, "His will be done." *In the Midst of This*, hopefully, we're on our way to relinquishing trying to control our situation by ourselves; trying to fix what only God can fix. For if you work too hard during your struggle, your struggle might be working you. It's far better to trust God's guidance to get the work done.

Be mindful that getting through anything is a process. I hope you have never thought or considered yourself to be so strong, courageous, and a no-nonsense type of Christian where getting through should be easy for you. If so, I hope you refrain from this kind of thinking. God has not told any of us to do everything by ourselves. He did say, however, that without Him, we can do nothing.

On the flip side, I pray you don't beat yourself up if you're not where you think you should be. Just know we will forever need God. We need His strength and power regardless of how strong we may think we are. For no one is strong enough to handle their *this* by themselves without dire repercussions. It is God who provides the strength by way of the Holy Spirit to get you and me through it all.

Never forget the Holy Spirit is our guide. He's ready to take on any challenge. Why not let Him! After all, nothing is too hard for Him. As stated before, He is also available to help us through those unexpected bad and miserable moments (BAM!). Be confident He's ever-present to show us clear biblical principles that will aid us in our situation while we're still going through.

He is also at hand to show us the value of prayer, how to worship God, and how to build our faith, trust, strength, and patience in Him. Not only that, He's here to encourage us to never stop worshipping and praising God from whom all our blessings flow.

I don't know about you, but when difficult times arise in my life, I now tend to think to myself, *Could it be that God is allowing my situation to linger to bring His purpose to pass? Could God be setting things in place to show forth His glory and power? Could God be preparing and strengthening my heart for what is to be*? When I think like this, I sense His calmness on the inside of me like the gentle waves of the sea. Then I rest.

I pray you are now mindful, regardless of how long it takes, that God is here, *in the midst of this process, to give us strength and rest . . . from being suppressed . . . by the stress of it all.* He is very present to demonstrate what we will need to gear up and face any challenge or hardship.

Therefore, I admonish you to keep on thanking and trusting God. Whether rain, shine, sleet or snow, God will never leave us in the midst of this, to bear it alone no matter where we roam.

Lastly, upon completion of reading this book, I pray you will be able to say, *in the midst of this, I will keep on gearing up and won't quit.* I can endure this trial through Christ, who is my guide and who gives me strength and a hope.

Special Note

By this time, I hope you understand how necessary it is to gear up or make ready in this world. Most importantly, for the world to come, have you geared up for the return of Christ by accepting Jesus as Lord and Savior? Have you made ready, *In the Midst of This*, for Him?

> *Therefore, stay awake, for you do not know on what day your Lord is coming.*
> —*Matthew 24:42*

About the Author

Hertistine was raised in a family with twelve siblings, she being the sixth oldest. She is a wife, mother, and grandmother. She is a faithful member of her church serving with various ministries.

Of Hertistine's many enjoyments in life, she especially takes joy in writing, water aerobics, spending time with family and friends, and working in her garden. Observing how plants grow and flowers bloom often reminds her of a special beauty God produces through nature to reflect His glory.

Having Christian parents, she was taught to always look to God as the source of her being. Raised on a plantation in the Mississippi Delta, Hertistine witnessed her parents working hard in the fields amidst other struggles. Around twelve, she, too, worked in the fields, chopping and picking cotton and, at times, staying home to see after younger siblings. Thus saying, during her early teenage years, she, too, became familiar with hard work, which gave her a firsthand experience of the many struggles her parents faced.

Being brought up in the church, she saw who her parents would call on in the midst of good times as well as tough times—God was the one, no matter how difficult things would get. Hertistine also noticed her parents' continued adoration of praise and worship to God despite how tight finances got and how low the food barrel became. They maintained their faith and trust that God would provide.

From their example, Hertistine had a godly foundation to base her life on; to never stop trusting God, look to Him for direction and guidance, trust God for the outcome as well as the journey and always express gratitude for what He has done.

Today, as she is no longer facing the hardships of living on a plantation, she realizes she is still living on the plantation of life with all its unexpected turns, hardships, difficulties, and sometimes overwhelming challenges. She understands she must always trust God in the midst of this.

Now grateful to be blessed with almost fifty years of marriage and having been through many of life's struggles, she still affirms God can be trusted.

In the Midst of This, Hertistine's faith is based on the principle God is more than capable to keep her by His grace, even as she is still going through some difficult times. With God, she still declares, "I can do all things through Christ who strengthens me," and so can you.

As the publication of *In the Midst of This* approaches, many of my fellow Los Angeles residents and those in surrounding areas have experienced aftereffects of devastating wildfires. I would like to express my sincere condolences to the families who have been impacted by the loss of loved ones and their homes. May the God of compassion, restoration, and love forever comfort, strengthen, and sustain you as you are still going through.